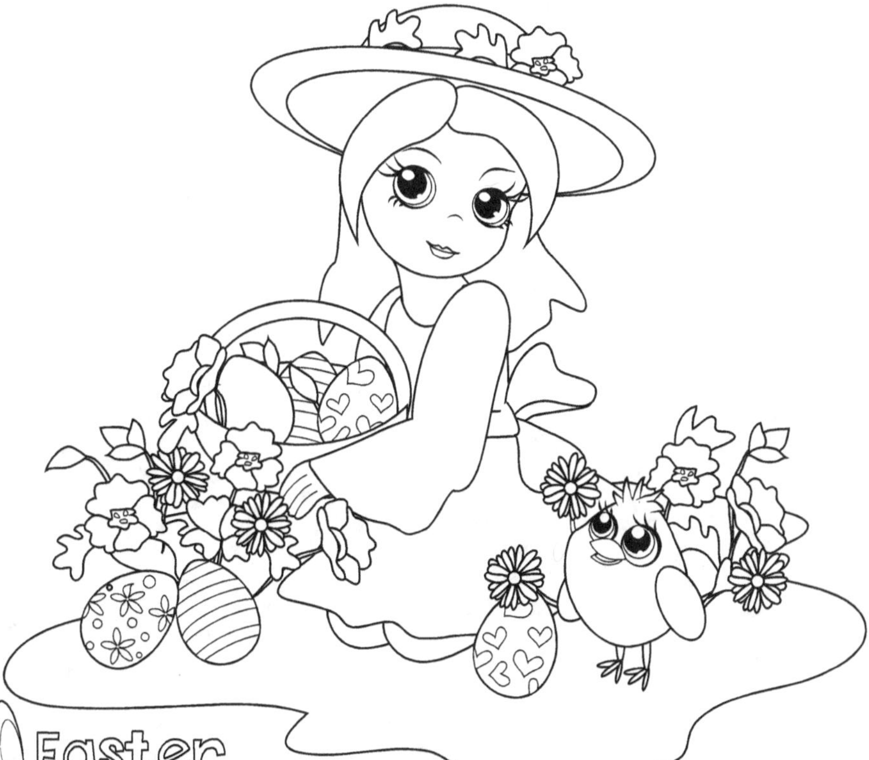

Easter Rabbit

THIS EASTER CARD BELONGS TO

My Magnificent Granddaughter:

____

Dear Granddaughter,
Good luck with your
Easter Egg hunt!

Wishing you the best holiday
with the cutest baby chicks.

Granddaughter's Bunny Poem

Bunnies are black,
Bunnies are white,
Bunnies are always,
An Easter delight!

I have a message for you
Granddaughter...
The Easter Bunny will be bringing
you so many yummy chocolates
because you are EGG-STRA special!

HOP TO THE NEXT EGG!

Enjoy this wonderful day filled with jelly beans, sweets, chocolates, and surprises for you!

You know it's Easter when there's fluffy little bunnies and sweet little treats.

Granddaughter...
You are more loved
Than a chocolate bunny!

Wishing a very magnificent
Granddaughter the best Easter possible!

Bunnies are cute,
Both big and small,
But I like the chocolate ones
Best of all! ~By Lusine

There is no other
Granddaughter
in the world who deserves
more sweets than you do!

How many chocolate lambs
can you eat in one day?

HAPPY EASTER
TO MY
MAGNIFICENT GRANDDAUGHTER!
COLORING CARD

We hope you've enjoyed this Easter Coloring Card.
Happy Easter!
florabellapublishing.com

Lots of hugs and kisses to you
this Easter!

Love,